She Needs That Edge
Paul Brookes

Nixes Mate Books
Allston, Massachusetts

Copyright © 2018 Paul Brookes

Book design by d'Entremont
Photo Paul Brookes

All rights reserved. This book or any portion thereof may not be reproduced or used in any manner whatsoever without the express written permission of the publisher except for the use of brief quotations in a book review or scholarly journal.

My grateful thanks to these magazines for previously publishing some of these poems: *Sacred Chickens*, and *Literati Magazine*

I am immensely grateful to Michael of Nixes Mate for accepting and publishing this work.

ISBN 978-0-9993971-0-7

Nixes Mate Books
POBox 1179
Allston, MA 02134
nixesmate.pub/books

For my late sister, Alison, a force of nature much missed.

Contents

In Answer To His Question   1
Their Mausoleum On His Fridge Door   17
She Is Seen As Unseen   23
She Needs That Edge   40
Their Hands Tell More Than Their Eyes   50

She Needs That Edge

In Answer To His Question

(i)

she pulls at the loose thread,
dries the pots on the draining board
hoovers the stray seed under the cage,
wipes the dusty blinds then raises them.
"I'm happy," she tells him.

(ii)

She sharpens her cheekbones,
creates light
highlights
diagonal from side of her nose
up to outer corner of her eye.
Light shade of concealer along the upper edges.
Matte bronzing powder under the bones
increases their height
for him.
"What do you think?"
she asks.

(iii)

She takes a hair out of his eye,
brushes dandruff from his collar,
loosens his tie, undoes top button
and second button of his shirt,
tidies the creases in his jacket,
pats dust off his shoulders,
and says "You look dapper, now",
as her fingers tuck her hair behind
her perfumed ear.

(iv)

She can still sense musk
she put on her neck earlier.
"I've got something in my eye.
Can you see it? You'll have to
move closer."
Her lace bra strap somehow comes loose.
"This shoe's killing me. Foots hard
and I've been too long in the saddle.
Not invading your space, love.
But can I use your shoulder while I straighten it out. "

(v)

blackbird jams to himself
on the non smoking chimney pot,
bright day emerges dazed,
officers still haven't found her body,
bluebells appear for the first time
along the railway embankment.
in the display window the bread is burnt,
she lets him touch her breast,
his hand stays there.

(vi)

The rains do not stop.
A ladder in her stockings
has rungs that multiply
when she crosses her legs.
His vape is losing flavour.
The little girl laughs as she leaps
the lines in the pavement.
He has used 80% of power
on his mobile.
An ant traverses breaks
in the concrete. The questioner
ogles the line of the waitresses legs
not hers
"Stop looking at her legs. You pervert."

(vii)

She crosses her legs
towards him:
the river in spate,
astroturf on the graves
needs a short back and sides.
She crosses her legs
away from him:
dust piles in forgotten corners,
babies lose their comfort blankets,
petals fall from the table vase.

(viii)

She separates items on her plate. Peas
from carrots, meat
from mash. Hot
from cold.
"How young we were when you asked me."
She folds her paper napkin into a crane
that nods.
She fold his into a T shirt.
"You've got to look in the right place."

(ix)

The waitress in a tiny black dress
has brought their food.
His hands are so soft and gentle
as he picks up the cold knife and fork,
she can only imagine the worst of it.
And decades ago:
A little girl in a gingham dress
rushes after a Yorkshire Terrier
who's strayed on the railway line.
A little boy reaches over the shining
pool full of his grandad's new
golden koi carp.
There were screams then, too.
"This mash is nice." she says.

(x)

Her wetwipe removes the gravy stain on his trousers,
"You'd never make a good criminal." she says.
At the other meal stains and crumbs are intentional.
Temptation is the first course.
Lure the innocent full spoon
with a promise or an adventure
into the quiver of a mouth .
The Act the main.
Unexpected threat.
Taste the screams.
Savour the dessert.
Admire the sweet iced silence
and/or the blood.
Coroners always so kind: "Death by Misadventure"
"Can't take you anywhere. You're worse
than a kid." she says.

xi)

Her late son and daughter's tender portraits
in the rare bloody meat on his plate,
arranged as when a child makes faces with its food.
His knife and fork separate threads
of their sinew and bone:
One bloated as if drowned.
The other in pieces as if smashed
by a speeding train.
Life defined by what is missing.
And then she sees
her own face there.
"Don't play with your food. Eat it properly." she scolds.
He makes her face in the meat smile.

(xii)

She tuts when he slaps his chops
and pulls at the strands of young life
caught between his incisors
and molars with his silvered tongue,
slurps bright cold beer from his pint glass,
mashes peas into mash, carrots
into Yorkshire pudding, oblivious
to what goes where and with what.
"All meets up in the same place, love"
she comments and laughs
and sees their graves
all in a row like teeth.

(xiii)

He always sups 11 pints of beer,
then stops. Has to reach
a certain level to be happy.
Their car is left at the pub.
She makes sure he gets home safely.
When they can't afford a taxi,
she oversees his wander:
into the road of fast cars,
other people's gardens to piss,
pokes him with her finger
to rouse his slumber,
and yanks a bush over himself
as if it were a bed blanket.
"Go onto half's," she recommends.
So he buys two halves, instead of a pint.

(xiv)

She smirks as he wipes his sloppy mouth
 with her origami napkin t shirt,
leaves a brown stain on the shirt sleeves,
slurps his ninth pint.
Watches him leer at the catwalking
long legged, black stockinged
waitress in her tiny black dress
as she carries his hot apple pie
and custard, and places before him
with a seductive, pouted "Enjoy." to his face,
and her cold fresh fruit salad.
She unfolds her origami napkin crane,
lays it on her lap, pauses an orange segment
before her dry mouth:
"We're walking home tonight.", she announces.

(xv)

Sips her black filter coffee as he downs
his last two pints and winks
at the waitress.
Outside it is a slight cold evening
he stumbles into the road
and raucous horns of drivers.
He dilly dallies, messes with his trousers.
She sees an Artic. gear toward him.
Rushes to ... and is held back by the tiny cold
hands of a little girl in a gingham
dress and a little boy.
"I can't. My kids." she shouts.
He screams. She watches the lorry kill him,
and the kids hands leave her.
Her dead kids disappear
into the sweet iced silence.

(xvi)

She stands in front of his tooth
of a gravestone. Cuts back the weeds,
scrubs the cheap Yorkshire stone.
She only puts roses on her little boy
and girl's graves as a thankyou.
"I'm happy." she tells them.

Their Mausoleum On His Fridge Door

(i)

His Heart Is Where Their Home Is
he tells himself in bold.
They live in a four room home
which is his heart.
Left atrium his wife's bedroom,
right atrium her office.
Left ventricle is his little boys
toy box of tractors
right ventricle is his little girls
card making factory.
His blood keeps their house
lubricated and his steady rhythm
beats through their working day.
They work and play from home.

(ii)

Tentatively, she examines the hole in her black stocking
clocks the eyes of young men who try to look askance
while she remembers grapes, adds them to her shopping
list and her mother's pigeon feet walk Hadrian's Wall
in the photo she'd sent from The Great Wall in China.

(iii)

Peels off the tissue as if it was a religious relic,
as she always insisted he leave no ragged edges
on the toilet or kitchen paper and shows the world
he is not lackadaisical and is his own man.

(iv)

Opens his fridge door to inhale the perfume
of her petal that rises before him.
Sun rises and sets over its white curve.
An approaching buzz makes him hurry back
inside the door of his globule of water
as his boiling kettle sounds like the fall of rain
yesterday. A bees proboscis sucks up his home
as he grasps the stalk that rises like a chimney out of it.

(v)

Sits down between the rimples of a freshly ploughed field,
grasps his wooden oars and sculls the plicas.
Hopes the turned soil will not capsize because he can't swim
great distances. His broadcast seed fell below the surface
of the waves he walked as now his wife and child
bob up and down between these dry rucks.

His oars are tissue paper flower petals.

(vi)

Mother in law walks the walls of his heart
sends post cards to his late wife of boundaries

she has hiked magnetically pinned to his fridge door.
A post it note that has lost it's stickiness and flaps

on the kitchen floor reminds him to tell his mother
in law his wife and kids drowned yesterday.

Longiforum lilies attract askance bees to their sacred
perfume chimneys.

(vii)

He sculls the ragged edged tissue paper of his heart's
    empty rooms.
His wife adjusts her stocking through the "I Love You
    Very Much"
purple words on the pale blue card held on his fridge door
by magnets featuring tractors in ploughed fields,
as water seeps out the worn seals of the defrosting fridge.
Soon his tissue oars will soak up all the water.

She Is Seen As Unseen

(i)

keeps to the dark of the tides,
so he keeps away from the riverside.

Every time she moves inland,
he wishes to be better lit.

Her breaths are not hidden.
Whisper arousal,

a swan's wing away from brokenness.

(ii)

laplap of waves in dry shadow under lintels
when he walks to work.

Historically the town has never been flooded.
River height engineered low as if an anger

held in check by self control.
Night to him is when the streets sway

under water, like weed.
And in the day

the lap of dark castor fibers gnaw willowbark
at water's edge, loosen sense so if the rains

come as before he will have no defence
in the deluge.

Her lightless body will smother
every hole in his body. He will

gasp for air, lungs so painful
he must find light to breathe.

(iii)

A harsh click. He imagines a moorhen,
then sees a brusque robin,

red chest on a white gargoyle
in a neglected garden,

with a mossy fence and high weed,
wilderness.

"A swinging brick for a heart.
Ericathus rubicula. Robin, love."

declares a woman in rollers
and black cat onesie

when she crosses his path
to put out a recycling bin.

(iv)

"Come in for a coffee. I've just brewed up."
"On my way to work."

"Call on your way home. I'll be in."
"I don't know you."

"You have an interest in birds is all I need to know "
"I could be a stalker. What's your mobile number?"

"Don't mess with those.
Google means go,ogle.

Portable masturbation devices,
bit of vibration, bit of titillation.

I'd rather ogle what's around me.
Get a feel, if I can.

Who would stalk this?"
She models her rollers, onesie and Muppet slippers.

(v)

He calls at her home after work,
to see a slim blonde spray tanned

young woman knelt down in tight pink
short shorts, and crop top plunge

a bright trowel
into the hard

weedful soil.
"Hi." she says "I'm Raquel."

"Kate said you might pop by.
So I said I give you a head

start. Shouldn't have got my
nails done. Blonde for a reason, eh!"

He sees the dark tide rise
in her pale blue eyes

hears the swan's wing
whisper arousal.

(vi)

A shout from the front door.
"Aye, my bush needs a trim.

You up to it?"
"Kate. You'll scare him off."

They laugh out loud.
He grins.

A little boy beside Kate
looks bemused.

"This is Jacob.
Raquel's mistake.

Go shake the man's
hand, then." she pushes

Jacob toward him.
"Come on in. Can't have

the neighbours saying
I'm not sociable,

and I'm sure you've ogled
enough of Raquel's nature

for now. Jacob, get in
you little scamp."

(vii)

He was glad their house number was 61.
It added up to 7, his favourite number.

In a morning he always did exercises.
20 arm swings. Touch toes once.

Lackadaisical on days adding up to four.
More focus. Be wary.

He always counted when taking medicines.
He knew it would go wrong

if he didn't count correctly.

(viii)

His dry migraine heave into the pan.
I don't need this. A hollow icy stomach.

Shot through with roll of her wild warm
darkest high swell over his inadequate

flood defences when they made
as if to hug, but resolved to shake hands

in the neglected garden. She sucked
him towards her, lifted him, then let

him fall. Adrift. Balance gone.
Skin's memory of her tender touch

fevers his blood. I don't need this.
She has found him, awash with her shadows,

smothers every chance for breath, blocks
all access to light, glowers above him,

and her swan's wing snaps his bones, one by one.
His dilated eyes make both women one.

(ix)

Raquel, and he can't bring himself
to say the name of her in the past

merge into one woman who loves him,
but gives him nothing but pain.

A nervous knock on the bathroom door.
"You alright, mister?" He answered

with a grunt. "Mam sent me to check."
"Dinner's ready." And footsteps down

the hall. Indistinct voices. The taste
of boiled new potatoes and cabbage.

Footsteps return. Soft knock.

"Are you a breast or leg man?

Mam says.

He takes a deep breath, counts

to seven and leaves the bathroom.

(x)

As he sits next to Jacob,
Kate announces "Gallus Gallus domesticus
hacked at by Raquel.
Breast or legs? Jacob never got a reply.
"Either or both." he says timidly.

" I like a man who likes a whole woman.
Doesn't break her down.
Into little parts like tits n' ass."
"Kate". admonishes Raquel with a wink,
and nod to Jacob.

"Excuse Kate's behaviour.
She comes on strong
when men's about."
"Excuse Raquel's coquettishness."

replied Kate. "This place is a Women's Refuge for
bored, abused
and lonely women.
Red or white? Wine.
Homemade. Plenty of.
Red, it is. Suck it up.
Bleed me dry, Raquel."

(xi)

It all seems to slip after the first bottle.
He can't remember.
Perhaps, Raquel took him upstairs
to sleep it off. Undressed him.
Put the covers over.
Undressed herself and slipped in.
He hears wings and his bones crack.
He can't breathe. Her thighs
either side of his head. Ripples,
then waves, then swell. He
drowns in her darkness.

(xii)

She always wakes before the alarm
on her mobile starts
and counts to seven. The alarm
is a recording of a German woman
bringing herself off.
"Raquel. Turn that down or off.
I've opened the windows. Not
everyone wants to hear
a German woman masturbating
first thing in the morning!" shouts
her companion Robin from the kitchen.

(xiii)

Raquel is bemused by her dreams.
In them she's always a man
who is killed by a woman called Raquel.

As dresses she glances at her notes
beside the bed: "Simultaneously
wave and particle, alive and dead,
ghost particles, energy transference,
male and female, swan's wing hypothesis."

Business lunch at "The Beavers Dam.
Recently unsandbagged. Historically,
The town has always been flooded.
She dresses for her body shape,
legs longer, breasts curvier, sharpens
her red lipstick, practises her smile,
her best asset: confidence.
All in the seeming, seem to make
the invisible visible, frivolous serious.

(xiv)

Over a morning coffee.
"You're all heart Robin",
"Mine's a swinging brick.
Clickety click."
her companion replies.

"What's yours, your Ladyship?"
"Drowning in swan's wings,
at the moment."

"Sock it to that little boy
of a boss, Jacob. Raq.
Don't let him run off."

(xv)

Dreams, better lenses, maps,
uncover better ways to see
the invisible. How can we
really see the people we know?

Access invisible knowledge.
Knowledge of the now gone,
or never seen, only known
through hints and shadows.

(xvi)

Raquel recalls her late sister Kate
finds a wishbone in her chicken,
holds one curved bone
in crook of her little finger,

offers Raquel the other
to hold likewise.
"Make a wish."
And now Raquel wishes
the future was known.

Kate gagged on her own vomit,
drunk and drugged up
Lovers Lane, while her male
companion survived. The bastard.

Grief is in the dark under lintels,
sometimes a ripple, then a wave,
then a swell lifts her up
makes her move in a small orbit
around it before return
to breathe in the light.

She Needs That Edge

(i)

She hates him making her safe.
Remembers times when she
searched

her pockets and the sofa
for fag money and the float

ten pound note she would give
to him and him to her when they were short.

"Life is boring when there's no edge to it." she says.

(ii)

"There should be summat to fight for!
Who needs an easy road,

without people and obstacles,
so there's nothing

to work around,
nothing to tell tales,

weep, wail and witter,
scrimp, scrape and scratter,

gripe, grieve and grapple about?"

(iii)

He wants the comfy chair,
in front of the TV.

All bills paid, no mortgage,
home fit to live in.

An easy going on.
Only he likes strong, passionate

women. They rearrange him,
upset, rattle and upside down him

with tirades about what
he hasn't done, what they think

he's done, what they think he's about.

(iv)

She'll do time
for next bloke

doles his fist
at her, on her, in her.

Next one who controls
like her mother.

Him, ligged out sozzled
on her sofa when

there's chores to be done.
Expects meat and two veg,

won't change his habits,
go places, do stuff.

(v)

You're mandled, mollycoddled.
Need to be chivied and mithered.

Too long seen you topple
your Mam and Dad grab

you up, smartish, to console.
Too much smothered

when deep in debt,
pulled out the mire,

dusted down and placed
on decent path, again.

Not fended and fought,
bended and bought,

mended your own path,
cleared undergrowth,

tramped and stamped
with your own sore feet.

No blisters and sores,
cuts and grazes you've picked

washed out ingrained grit,
gravel while grimaced.

(vi)

And he would say if he could:
"Not everyone's your mother!

Not everyone's after making
you miscarry that faith in yourself.

Pregnant with youthful confidence,
she had you haul her heavy boned

bloated hatred that you were ever born
from room to room, up

and down steep stairs to inflict
a bloody carcass on your womb.

You did as she asked but ensured
that little bairn gave

you a reason to go on.
A clear eye to nurture.

A warmth to cuddle.
A life to save."

(vii)

"I'm not going to seed
sat on my arse.

Alzheimer fodder.
Comfort zones are killing zones.

Once, I was hard as nails.
You're useless.

Used to be someone
to butt up against.

Challenge me.
You've made me soft, and I've let you.

Never knew how exhausted
I was. Batteries recharged.

I'll stay with you, for now.
A daily reminder

of what I don't need.
I need a gun to my head.

A knife at my throat.
I'll put me back

in the fire.

Their Hands Tell More Than Their Eyes

(i)

She read her first hands.
Small, spatula shaped.

Stumpy fingers.
Not large enough to be manual.

Not thin enough to be artistic.
Wanted to be a true reflection

of others, but his surface
held too many imperfections.

His eyes were blank spheres,
his conflict in his palms.

He would lie to her.
Keep things to himself.

He gave her doubt.

(ii)

Another's long tender digits play timpani
between her legs. Their slender

reach

works a flood within her
as they helter skelter

spirals from tip to base
on each of her breasts.

She loses control when
they are half way down

the slide and she flies.
His tongue: a ninth finger,

touch types her labia
so she breathes glossolalia

with her ninth finger
He made her feel good.

(iii)

Another: more fish than man.

His skin has scales
between his fingers,

at their base
a thin film to make

any swim easier.
His imagination is a fish bladder.

He swerves over her coral.
She saw another way to live.

(iv)

She examines her hands in awe,

as if newly discovered.
Amazed they belong to her,

and that she controls them.
Curls each finger, notes

how each joint works.
Finger of one hand follows

the lines of the other
as if to remap, re traverse

the landscapes of age.
She let her know what was to come.

(v)

In the purple blossom
of her bruises

she traces the shape
of his knuckles.

Cries at the glad fall
into the gentle browns

of his eyes, strength
of his black hair.

She learns how to leave,
how to say "no".

(vi)

His wife has chocolate fingers,
dark and sweet,

inhale bubblegum
from the tips,

pink wafer nails,
taste of red fruit wine.

A taste that doesn't cloy,
not syrupy or over sugared.

This woman knows how to work her fingers.

(vii)

Daddy God finger, abuse finger, where are you?
Here I am, here I am, let me do you, let me do you.

Mummy Mary finger, let him finger, where are you?
Here I am, here I am. Let him do you. Let him do you.

Brother finger, Cain finger, where are you?
Here I am, Here I am, ready to kill, ready to kill.

Sister finger, Mercy finger, where are you?.
Here I am, Here I am, Pray to you, pray to you.

Baby finger, Jesus finger, where are you?
Here I am, here I am. Killed for you, killed for you.

Graspy thumb, toolly thumb, where are you?
Here I am. Here I am. Work for you, work for you.

(viii)

Tiny lamb's hooves gain purchase
in the grooves of gust worn cracks

beneath a looming ancient stone crag.
Little fingers like young stones caught,

in the raked valleys of a Zen garden,
a tiny baby grasps Dad's finger base ,

cranes eyes to the precipice edge ,
the furrowed horizon of skin.

(ix)

Her hand is a military formation.
Four sharp spears stand upright,

stab forward,
curl with the thumb

into a bony shield,
of knuckles.

Too much like his.

(x)

His loam palms,
carrot fingers,

parsnip thumbs,
bring harvest

over our threshold.
Sustenance.

(xi)

His butter fingers
massage themselves

into her body
until he is no more

and she glows
with oil of him.

He makes her shine.

(xii)

"Best left till late in life."
He says "So many nerve

endings when you get it done.
And near the knuckle

for other folk as you can't
really keep them hid."

Wide awake turquoise eyes
of his late wife, one

per hand follow me
round the room.

"She was always one
for eyeing up other blokes."
he says.

(xiii)

Twenty canvasses of your own.
Each nail is a canvas.

Even two year olds daub
them with a tiny brush.

On every high street two or three
businesses compete cuticles.

No airheads chewing gum,
buffing nails and passing calls.

Operating theatre masks,
nail drying machines by their side.

French or gel.
Indulged luxury in austerity.

At home sisters bond and learn
techniques of togetherness.

If you do mine, I'll do yours.
Choose colour or tattoo.

Delicacy of touch and focus.
Mindfulness colouring book.

Pampered by laughter
and forgetting.

(xiv)

Nanna has no time for nails.
Forever pegs out on washing,

Her hands turn, twist,
push and pull, grind and grist,

make meals, scrub thresholds.
poss dirt, brush soot, polish tiles,

learn to live with bruises, blebs,
blisters, blemishes, bleeds,

mangle water, wring an easier
going on until convenience saves time.

(xv)

Grandad's hands are made
of coal dust, and steel shavings.

Layers of ancient trees, molten
pig runs through his veins.

Lathe turned, tool maker palms
cradle call centre headset

in environmentally controlled
warehouse where he negotiates

customer complaints while
his hands grow soft his brain

works out, solution led,
business aligned conundrums.

(xvi)

Learn to read your own hands.
Family history in fingerprint ridges.

Smell yesterdays meals, how
seasons of heat and cold ingrain

in lines like longitude and latitude.
Like rocks weathered by smoke,

yellowed by tobacco stains, reddened
by beetroot, oranged by carrots.

Blue black pen stain from school.
Scars of damage with stories attached.

You must use your eyes to see
your hands tell more than your eyes.

About the Author

Paul Brookes was, and is, a shop assistant, after employment as a security guard, postman, admin. assistant, lecturer, poetry performer with "Rats for Love". His latest book, *A World Where*, was published by Nixes Mate Books. His work was included in *Rats for Love: The Book*, (Bristol Broadsides, 1990). He has published the chapbooks *The Fabulous Invention Of Barnsley*, (Dearne Community Arts, 1993), the illustrated *The Headpoke And Firewedding* (Alien Buddha Press), and the illustrated *The Spermbot Blues* (OpPRESS) He has read his work on BBC Radio Bristol and designed and presented a writer's workshop for sixth formers that was broadcast on Radio Five Live. More of him can be found at
https://thewombwellrainbow.wordpress.com/

Nixes Mate Books features small-batch artisanal literature, created by writers that use all 26 letters of the alphabet and then some, honing their craft the time-honored way: one line at a time.

Other or Forthcoming Nixes Mate titles:

WE ARE PROCESSION, SEISMOGRAPH | Devon Balwit
ON BROAD SOUND | Rusty Barnes
JESUS IN THE GHOST ROOM | Rusty Barnes
CAPP ROAD | Matt Borczon
HE WAS A GOOD FATHER | Mark Borczon
THE WILLOW HOWL | Lisa Brognano
A WORLD WHERE | Paul Brookes
SQUALL LINE ON THE HORIZON | Pris Campbell
MY SOUTHERN CHILDHOOD | Pris Campbell
A FIRE WITHOUT LIGHT | Darren C. Demaree
LABOR | Lisa DeSiro
KINKY KEEPS THE HOUSE CLEAN | Mari Deweese
AIR & OTHER STORIES | Lauren Leja
HITCHHIKING BEATITUDES | Michael McInnis
SMOKEY OF THE MIGRAINES | Michael McInnis
THE LIVES OF ATOMS | Lee Okan
LUBBOCK ELECTRIC | Anne Elezabeth Pluto
STARLAND | Jessica Purdy
WAITING FOR AN ANSWER | Heather Sullivan
COMES TO THIS | Jeff Weddle
HEART OF THE BROKEN WORLD | Jeff Weddle
NIXES MATE REVIEW ANTHOLOGY 2016/17

nixesmate.pub/books

www.ingramcontent.com/pod-product-compliance
Lightning Source LLC
Chambersburg PA
CBHW052135010526
44113CB00036B/2260